# Who Is Pope Francis?

WITHDRAWN

by Stephanie Spinner

illustrated by Dede Putra

Penguin Workshop
An Imprint of Penguin Random House

For Richard Straub, who is saintly—SS

To the memory of my dad, who always supported
me to pursue my dream—DP

PENGUIN WORKSHOP
Penguin Young Readers Group
An Imprint of Penguin Random House LLC

Copyright © 2017 by Penguin Random House LLC. All rights reserved. Published by Penguin Workshop, an imprint of Penguin Random House LLC, 345 Hudson Street, New York, New York 10014. PENGUIN and PENGUIN WORKSHOP are trademarks of Penguin Books Ltd. WHO HQ & Design is a registered trademark of Penguin Random House LLC. Printed in the USA.

*Library of Congress Cataloging-in-Publication Data is available.*

ISBN 9780451533364 (paperback)          10 9 8 7 6 5 4 3 2 1
ISBN 9780451533388 (library binding)     10 9 8 7 6 5 4 3 2 1

# Contents

Who Is Pope Francis? . . . . . . . . . . . . . . . . . . 1

A Close Family . . . . . . . . . . . . . . . . . . . 6

Becoming a Priest . . . . . . . . . . . . . . . . . . 15

Changes . . . . . . . . . . . . . . . . . . . . . . 30

A Changed Man . . . . . . . . . . . . . . . . . . 46

Choosing a Pope . . . . . . . . . . . . . . . . . . 55

Shocking News . . . . . . . . . . . . . . . . . . 68

A New Day . . . . . . . . . . . . . . . . . . . 76

A Helping Hand . . . . . . . . . . . . . . . . . 84

Taking Charge . . . . . . . . . . . . . . . . . . 89

A Church of the Heart . . . . . . . . . . . . . 98

Timelines . . . . . . . . . . . . . . . . . . . 104

Bibliography . . . . . . . . . . . . . . . . . . 106

# Who Is Pope Francis?

One day Jorge Mario Bergoglio was on his way to meet some friends. (Say: HOAR-hay MAH-ree-oh bear-GO-lyo). But instead he stopped suddenly and then turned around. He walked into his neighborhood church in Buenos Aires, Argentina. He told the priest that he wanted to devote his life to God. Jorge was only sixteen years old at the time. He hadn't planned his words.

They surprised him, yet they were completely heartfelt. From that moment on they shaped his life.

Today Jorge Mario Bergoglio is known as Pope Francis, leader of the Roman Catholic Church. Ever since he became pope in 2013, Francis has worked to help the poor. Again and again, he delivers a message to everyone, not only Catholics, of hope and joy.

Some say he will make important changes to the Catholic Church. This may happen or it may not. Either way, Pope Francis's faith still shapes every day of his life. And it inspires people everywhere.

# Who Is the Pope?

The pope is the leader of the Catholic Church. The first pope was Peter, one of Jesus's twelve followers. Because of his faith, Peter was killed by the Roman emperor Nero in the year 67. Many more popes were killed during the days of the

Statue of St. Peter

Roman Empire. But in 313, the emperor Constantine recognized Christianity as a religion and became a Christian himself. After that, the papacy (the job of being pope) became a lot safer.

By the Middle Ages, Catholicism had spread throughout Europe, and the Church was extremely powerful. Back then, being a pope was like being an emperor. Popes could call up armies and lead them. They could appoint kings. They could hire great

The inside of St. Peter's Basilica

artists to build and decorate magnificent cathedrals. They could lead lives of great luxury.

Today the pope is still the final authority on all questions of morals and faith. Catholics are expected to obey him on matters of religion. Modern popes have worked with the United Nations and addressed the US Congress. They meet with presidents, queens, and kings. But they are not political leaders; they are spiritual leaders.

# CHAPTER 1
## A Close Family

Jorge Mario Bergoglio was born in South America—in Buenos Aires, Argentina—in 1936.

Jorge

His parents, Mario and Regina, were part of the city's large Italian community. Like their neighbors, they were hardworking people who spoke Italian at home and went to church often. Argentina was a Catholic country, and this was important to the Bergoglios. It made their new home feel a little like their old one.

Jorge was the oldest of five children. He was close to his parents and to his brothers and sisters. But the person who knew him best was his grandmother Rosa. Outspoken and warm, she took care of little Jorge during the day. She taught him about the Catholic saints, prayed with him, and took him to church. She also taught him to be open-minded. Her acceptance of people, whether they were Catholic or not, was something Jorge never forgot.

Rosa also taught Jorge to love books. He was fascinated by the Italian novels she read to him, with their dramatic stories and many characters. And he looked forward to Saturday afternoons when the family gathered to listen to Italian opera on the radio.

Jorge was an excellent student who worked hard in school. Yet as much as he enjoyed his studies, Jorge loved soccer more. He followed the sport closely with his friends and longed to be a great player. He settled for being a lifelong fan. Even as pope, he is still a member of the Buenos Aires soccer club of his boyhood. And when the team plays a game, he always knows the score.

Jorge and his brothers and sisters went to Catholic schools. Every evening after their father, Mario, came home from work, he led the family in prayer. Their priest, Don Enrico Pozzoli, was a friend as well. He often came for dinner to eat Rosa's delicious homemade ravioli.

The Bergoglio family lived in a city where many young men entered the priesthood. So Jorge's decision to become a priest was not unusual. It certainly did not surprise his grandmother Rosa, who knew him so well.

Jorge's parents were another matter. They had expected him to continue his studies in chemistry. His mother had always hoped Jorge would become a doctor. With a medical degree, he would have a comfortable life. He would never have to worry about money the way she and Mario did. Being a priest also meant that Jorge would never marry or have children. Though Don Enrico did his best to change her mind, it was years before Regina could accept her son's decision.

Diocesan Seminary of Villa Devoto

Yet Jorge was determined. In 1956, he enrolled at a seminary—a school for future priests—in Buenos Aires.

# CHAPTER 2
# Becoming a Priest

Many of Jorge's teachers at the seminary belonged to the Jesuit order. Jesuits are known as scholars. Jorge decided he wanted to become a Jesuit, too.

But doing that took long years of training and study—ten years to become a priest and another three or four to become a full member of the order.

So it was not a decision that Jorge made lightly. And before he was able to act on it, he became so ill that he almost died.

In August 1957, he came down with a very serious lung disease. Medicine didn't cure it, and he was soon struggling to breathe. He had to have part of his right lung removed. He then spent a month in the hospital in terrible pain.

Jorge's health had always been good. Now, for the first time in his life, he was suffering. His pain was hard to bear, but it made him understand the suffering of others in the world. And it strengthened his desire to devote his life to God. During his long recovery, he talked often with Don Enrico. The priest encouraged him to study with the Jesuits. When he was well again, Jorge applied to the Jesuit academy. He was accepted to begin his studies the following spring.

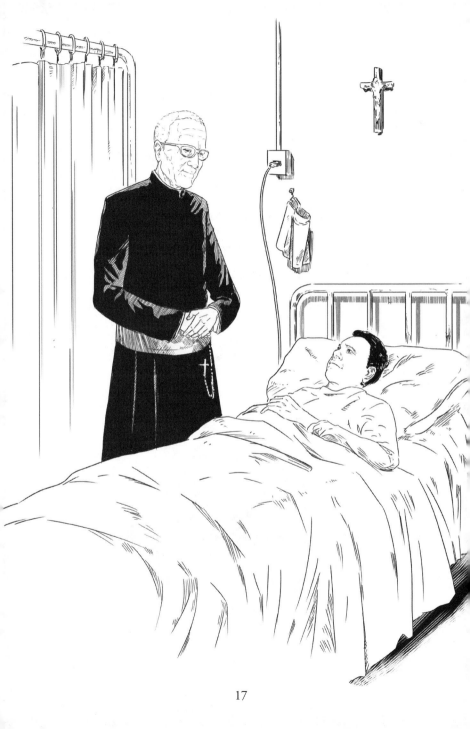

# The Jesuits

The Jesuit order is also called the Society of Jesus. It began with Ignatius of Loyola, a sixteenth-century Spanish nobleman. Loyola was not a religious man. But in 1521, while recovering from a battle wound, he read books about the lives of Jesus and the saints. They made him think his own life lacked meaning.

Ignatius of Loyola

One night he had a vision of the Virgin Mary, the mother of Jesus. It brought him great happiness.

Loyola was a changed man after that. He traveled through Europe without money and prayed for fifteen years. In 1548, he published a book that told how to lead a truly spiritual life. Doing good in the world, living without money or power, and always being ready to serve God are the basic requirements. The Jesuit order is founded on them. Ignatius of Loyola was made a saint in 1622.

Today the order is renowned for its thousands of schools. With more than seventeen thousand members, it is the largest order in the Catholic Church.

Jorge's training began in 1958 in Buenos Aires. Like the other new Jesuit students (called novices), he spent his first two years praying and studying according to the rules set by St. Ignatius of Loyola. Jorge took part in a monthlong silent retreat with the other novices. He did hospital work

with the sick and dying. At the seminary, he did household tasks like sweeping and laundry. He also taught in local schools.

His day began at 6:20 in the morning and ended at 10:30 at night. There was no free time; his entire day was spent working, studying, or praying. He also had to search his conscience three times a day. That meant he would think carefully about how he behaved and whether he could have done better. Every so often, he and his fellow novices gathered for a meeting called the culpa. The novice master would choose one of the student priests. Then all the others had to tell him what he had been doing wrong.

The other novices thought Jorge was very serious. In fact, he was even criticized for being a little too serious in the culpa. Jorge took this in stride. If he had any doubts about his faith, he kept them to himself and tried to overcome them.

In March 1960, he took his first vows of poverty, chastity, and obedience. Vowing poverty meant he would live simply. Vowing chastity meant he would never get married or have a romantic relationship with anyone. Vowing obedience meant he would always obey the word of God and the pope. Taking these first vows meant Jorge Mario Bergoglio was now a Jesuit priest, and could add the letters SJ, for Society of Jesus, to his name.

Even so, he had to train and study for many more years before he was fully ordained.

In 1961, Jorge went to a Jesuit school in Santiago, Chile, to study art, history, literature, and philosophy (the study of the meaning of life). While he was there, his father, Mario, died suddenly of a heart attack. Only weeks later, his longtime friend Don Enrico died also. Jorge mourned both men deeply. They had loved and encouraged him. Even more important,

they had taught him to respect and love all human beings.

Jorge thought of his father and Don Enrico often while he was in Chile, especially when he was teaching religion to third- and fourth-grade children. He had seen poverty in Argentina. But life for the poor in Chile was much worse. Jorge was shocked by what he saw.

His pupils had next to nothing. They often went hungry. They wore rags, and some didn't even own shoes. Jorge's heart went out to them. By the time he left Chile, his love and understanding for the poor had grown even stronger. It influences much of what he says and does as pope.

In 1963, Jorge returned to Argentina. He earned a degree in philosophy. After that he taught at the best Catholic high schools in Buenos Aires. At one of them—the Colegio del Salvador—he invited the great Argentinian writer Jorge Luis Borges to come for a visit (say: BORE-hays). Borges was famous—he would later win the Nobel Prize in Literature. Yet he was

Jorge Luis Borges

happy to come. For five days he read his work to the students. He also helped them with their own writing. He talked to them about the rugged life of the gauchos (Argentine cowboys), which had inspired many of his stories.

When word got out that Borges was at the school, teachers, pupils, and admirers flocked to hear him. One teacher said it was like hiring the best orchestra in the world to play "Happy Birthday" at a children's party! It was an experience Jorge would always treasure.

# CHAPTER 3
## Changes

Jorge's students admired him because he was a brilliant teacher with an excellent sense of humor. He was dedicated to them. He also knew that outside the medieval stone walls of the Colegio, changes in the Catholic Church were coming fast.

From 1962 to 1965, Catholic religious leaders from dozens of countries gathered in Rome for a series of religious meetings. It was called the Second Vatican Council (or Vatican II). Its purpose was to discuss the Catholic Church's role in the modern world. Some felt strongly that the Church should work to make the world a better place. Others wanted to make the Church more modern. For example, the Mass and other Church rituals had always been said in Latin.

Second Vatican Council (Vatican II)

That was because during the early years of the Catholic Church, educated people read and wrote in Latin. But by the 1960s, most people didn't study it or understand it.

Vatican II allowed the native language of each country to be used in church instead of Latin. This was a big change. It made rituals and prayers much easier for Catholics to understand.

Another result of Vatican II was to make the Catholic Church more accepting of other religions. For much of its history, Catholicism had claimed to be the only "true" religion. All others were considered inferior—not as good. After Vatican II, Catholic officials began to meet with Protestant, Jewish, and Muslim spiritual leaders in hopes of fostering friendship.

While Vatican II was taking place, Jorge followed the news from Rome closely. He believed the Church was changing for the better, bringing religion closer to the people. As pope, this is still one of his main goals.

During the 1960s, Argentina's government was also changing. They were years of unrest, when different political groups fought for power. Some represented the workers, others the military (the army, navy, and air force). The military usually won. General Juan Carlos Ongania seized leadership in 1966 and became dictator—

General Juan Carlos Ongania

what he said was law. He ran the country until 1970. Two more military dictators came after him, and their rule was equally harsh.

Then, in 1973, Juan Perón was reelected president. Perón had already held office from 1946 to 1955. His many followers hoped that his return would improve life in Argentina. But he died within the year, and when his wife, Isabel, took his place, she was quickly overthrown. In 1976, Argentina once again fell into the hands of the military. It was the beginning of a very

Juan Perón

dark time in its history. Argentinians called it "the Dirty War."

Through these uncertain years of political change, Jorge's life changed also. In 1973, he took his final vows as a Jesuit priest. Soon after, he became head of the Colegio del Salvador's Department of Philosophy and Theology.

Colegio del Salvador

That same year, when he was thirty-six years old, he was made a Jesuit provincial superior. This meant he was in charge of all the Jesuits in Argentina and neighboring Uruguay.

In his new position, Jorge worked hard to help the poor. He supported the Jesuits who worked in the slums of Buenos Aires and in other poor areas of the country. He opened new churches. And time after time he spoke about reaching out to those he called "God's faithful people."

Jorge did many worthwhile things as provincial, but he made decisions quickly, and by himself. If his ideas were unpopular with other Jesuits, he didn't care. By insisting that he knew best, he made enemies.

He made more enemies when he didn't speak out against the military dictatorship (called the junta). The junta was a group of three top military men: one from the army,

The Junta

one from the navy, and one from the air force.
They had enormous power. They killed tens of
thousands of people—anyone they thought was
opposing them. Argentinians called these victims
*los desaparecidos*, "the disappeared," because so
many vanished without a trace.

Some Jesuit priests wanted to demonstrate
against the junta. Jorge thought it was a bad idea
and ordered them to keep silent. A few disobeyed

him and protested openly. They were quickly jailed and held in prison for years without a trial.

The fact that Jorge never opposed the junta drew fierce criticism. People brought it up after the Dirty War ended in 1983, and later in 2013 when he became pope. He admits that he made mistakes, and he regrets them. "I had to deal with difficult situations, and I made my decisions abruptly and by myself. . . . My authoritarian and quick manner of making decisions led me to have serious problems and to be accused of being ultraconservative." (By *ultraconservative*, he meant someone who supported the junta.)

But Pope Francis has also revealed that he worked behind the scenes to save people from the junta. He secretly allowed dozens who were in danger of arrest to hide in the Jesuits' headquarters. He arranged for many to escape from Argentina to Europe. These were highly risky things to do. If he had been found out, he would have been thrown into prison, or worse. Luckily, that didn't happen.

Jorge's term as Jesuit provincial ended in 1980. By then, the priests who disliked him could stop his rise in the Jesuit order—and they did. Jorge was told to go back to teaching and then finish his doctorate in theology. (A doctorate is the highest degree a person can get in any subject.) After working on it briefly in Germany, he returned to Argentina, moving from one university to another as ordered.

In 1990, he was sent to live in the Jesuit residence in Córdoba, far from Buenos Aires. Here he was not allowed to teach, or to say Mass, or even to make phone calls without permission. For someone who had been in charge, it was harsh punishment for his unpopular actions.

Jorge had taken a vow of obedience, and now it was being tested. So he earned his doctorate. He spent time with the poor people of Córdoba. And he thought long and hard about his faith.

# The Clergy:
# Who Does What in the Catholic Church

Priests are men who devote their lives to the Church. Most have college degrees. They then go on to study in a Catholic seminary for another four to five years. Priests take special vows, in which they promise to follow Church rules. They lead religious ceremonies, such as the Mass. They baptize and marry people. They preach sermons and oversee funerals.

They hear confessions. They may also teach or do missionary work—that means traveling to other parts of the world to bring the Catholic faith to new people. Priests usually live with other priests in a group home and work in a Catholic district called a parish. Parish priests are supervised by a bishop.

Priests can also choose to join an order, like the Jesuits or the Franciscans.

Bishops are priests who are selected to become Church leaders. They are put in charge of a group of parishes, called a diocese. Bishops are thought of as part of a chain that began with Jesus's twelve followers. There are about five thousand bishops in the world right now.

Archbishops are chosen by the pope to lead very large dioceses, such as those in big cities. Pope Francis served as the archbishop of Buenos Aires from 1998 to 2013.

Cardinals are bishops hand-picked by the pope to be his advisers. As a group they are called the College of Cardinals. Their most important job is to elect the next pope. There are about two hundred cardinals.

Their red hats are symbols of their loyalty to the Church, meaning that they would shed blood to defend it.

The pope is the leader of the whole Catholic Church. He is also called the Bishop of Rome, the Supreme Pontiff of the Universal Church, and the Vicar of Jesus Christ.

# CHAPTER 4
## A Changed Man

In 1992, Jorge's years of punishment ended. The Jesuits had come to see that he was a man with special talents. That year he was appointed to help the archbishop of Buenos Aires run all the Catholic churches in the city. It was a demanding job, but Jorge seemed happy with his new responsibilities. After many years of humble work and soul-searching, he had changed. Now he listened carefully to people working with him. He made a point of talking with them before making decisions. And he focused even more on helping the poor.

At the time, there were about three million people in Buenos Aires. More than eight hundred thousand were very poor. They lived on less than a dollar or two a day. They had little electricity and no running water. Jobs were scarce, and the pay was very low. The crime rate was high. So was drug use.

The slums became Jorge's target. He sent more priests there. He helped to raise money for soup kitchens and schools. And he often went there himself. They were crowded, dirty, dangerous places, but he never took a bodyguard. As he walked around, he talked to everyone he met.

Jorge became archbishop in 1998. Most archbishops live in luxury. But silk robes, limousines, a big house, and first-class travel didn't interest Jorge. He wore ordinary robes and a plain cross. He lived in a small apartment. He cooked for himself. He rode a bicycle or took the subway to work. He had taken a vow of poverty and he was living by it, just as he always had.

Jorge's way of doing things set a powerful example for his fellow priests. It showed that the Catholic Church was truly dedicated to helping people in need. And it won him great affection in the city's poorest neighborhoods. There, they nicknamed him "the dude."

Admiration for Jorge grew during the late 1990s. The economy in Argentina was in terrible trouble. When the peso became almost worthless, and millions of Argentinians fell into poverty,

Jorge spoke out in his sermons (the speeches he gave during Mass). He criticized the government for borrowing too much money from foreign countries, and for cutting thousands of jobs in Argentina. He spoke out against dishonest, greedy officials for misleading the public. He also led talks between politicians and citizens' groups. His courage, and his willingness to work hard to ease the crisis, impressed many people.

In Rome, John Paul II, who was pope at the time, heard about Jorge's work, and approved. He made Jorge a cardinal in 2001. In the Catholic Church, only the pope can bestow this honor. Cardinals have great authority. They are the highest-ranking Church officials under the pope, and they are the ones who elect a new pope.

Jorge flew to Rome by himself for the ceremony. He didn't want friends or family to come along. He told them to give their travel money to the poor instead.

When he returned to Buenos Aires, Jorge continued to live simply. He would not wear red silk robes, as most cardinals do. He stayed in his little apartment. And he kept visiting the poor in the slums. He also visited city hospitals every week, speaking with very sick and dying patients, and blessing them. During one visit in 2001, he washed the feet of patients infected with HIV, the virus that causes AIDS. It was such an unusual act of humility for an important Church leader that many newspapers wrote about it.

"Society forgets the sick and the poor," he told reporters. His message was clear: Society might forget the sick and the poor, but the Church did not. It put them first.

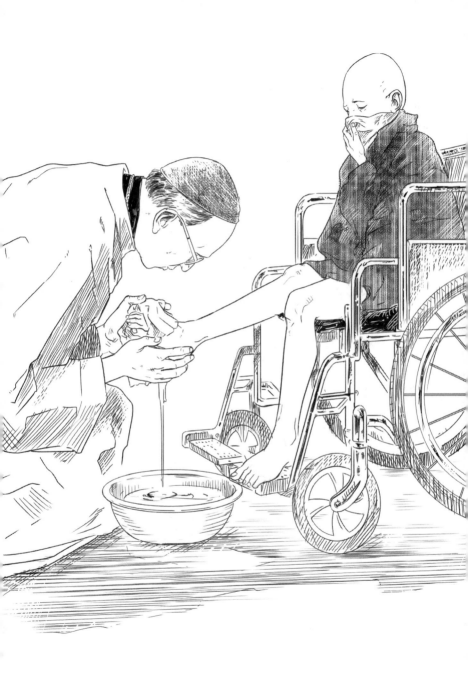

As a cardinal, Jorge also worked to unify the Jesuit order. In Argentina, it had broken into opposing groups during the Dirty War. He hadn't been able to bring those groups together while he was a Jesuit provincial. But he was humbler now. He no longer acted as if he alone had the right answer. And he was much better at giving people advice. With his help, the Jesuit brothers finally were able to bury their differences and work together.

The new cardinal was not only humble, he was a strong leader.

# CHAPTER 5
## Choosing a Pope

Ever since Vatican II, the Catholic Church had struggled to become more modern. Many other religions had been giving women positions of authority. Jewish women could now become rabbis. Protestant women could become ministers.

But in the Catholic Church, only men could become priests. And the Church would not approve of divorce or gay marriage. At the same time, it ignored or even hid the mistakes and crimes of its own clergy. As a result, hundreds of thousands of Catholics had been leaving the Church every year, and it was failing to attract new members.

Pope John Paul II had always wanted to make the Church more open. During his

Pope John Paul II

Pope John Paul II with leaders from other religions

twenty-five years as pontiff, he had encouraged Catholics to accept people of all religions. And he made many patient attempts to break down barriers of ignorance, mistrust, and hatred.

# Nuns

Catholic nuns are women who, like priests, devote their lives to the Church. They, too, take solemn vows of poverty, chastity, and obedience. Long ago all nuns lived apart from the rest of the world, praying, eating, and working together. In time, they began to do more in the outside world.

They might live in a convent—a special house with a chapel—but work in society as nurses or teachers. Today nuns help poor and elderly people, orphans, prisoners, and refugees. And they travel far and wide to open Catholic schools and missions.

Nuns cannot say Mass or hear confession. Yet their strong faith and tireless charitable work have made them a powerful force in the Church.

Jorge greatly admired the pope. So like millions of Catholics worldwide, he mourned deeply when Pope John Paul II died on April 2, 2005. Two weeks later, Jorge and 114 other cardinals traveled to Rome to choose a new pope. The gathering, called a papal conclave, was governed by many rules, some centuries old.

The cardinals had to take a vow of secrecy before they voted. They had to remain inside the Sistine Chapel at the Vatican until there was an election. To become pope, a cardinal needed a two-thirds majority—in this case, more than seventy-six votes. Voting could go on for a long time.

# Vatican City

Vatican City in Rome, Italy, is the world headquarters of the Catholic Church. It is also a tiny independent country ruled by the pope. About 1.5 square miles, it has a flag, an anthem, a central bank, and a postal system. It prints its own money and postage stamps, and issues license plates and passports. It even has an army called the Swiss Guard—the smallest army in the world.

At the center of Vatican City is St. Peter's Basilica. This enormous church was first a shrine to protect St. Peter's grave. The design and construction of the current Basilica, which was finished in 1626, took more than a hundred years to complete.

St. Peter's Basilica

Millions and millions of people visit Vatican City every year. They come to see the pope, who speaks

from a balcony every week. If they are lucky, he will invite them to ride around St. Peter's Square with him in his little "Popemobile."

The Sistine Chapel is the place in Vatican City where cardinals gather to choose a new pope.

On April 18, 2005, a huge crowd gathered in St. Peter's Square in Vatican City. People had come from all over the world for this event.

As the day wore on, they watched the Sistine Chapel chimney. A plume of black smoke would mean that so far no cardinal had won. A plume of white smoke would mean there was a new pope. Twice that day, and once the next, the smoke coming from the chimney was black.

Then, in the afternoon of the second day, a plume of white smoke finally arose. Minutes later, the bells of the Sistine Chapel rang out, signaling the welcome news. There was a new pope! The crowd wept and cheered. As they rejoiced, a small, white-haired man appeared on a balcony high above the square. Formerly Cardinal Joseph Ratzinger of Germany, he was now the 265th pope in history. And at seventy-eight, he was one

of the oldest ever chosen. He had taken the name Benedict—the sixteenth pope to take this name.

When he stepped forward a hush fell over the square. Pope Benedict XVI gave the crowd his blessing.

John Paul had been pope for more than twenty-five years. Benedict's time as Holy Father would be very short.

# CHAPTER 6
## Shocking News

When Jorge left Rome after the 2005 conclave, he knew that many cardinals had voted for him to be pope. (Voting was supposed to be secret, but information had a way of getting out.) By the fourth round of voting he was in second place, with forty votes out of the required seventy-seven.

But he was not interested in becoming the pope. He was already making plans to retire. When he did, he would live in a little apartment building in Buenos Aires with other retired priests. So during the conclave he had urged his fellow cardinals to vote for the new Pope Benedict, and they had.

After his election, Pope Benedict XVI led the

Church through some very difficult times. There were scandals over priests who got to keep their jobs even when they did not deserve to. Catholics around the world were leaving their parish churches in large numbers. Many who stayed were demanding reform—change for the better. There had always been priests who argued for reform, too. Now their number was growing.

Meanwhile, Jorge turned seventy-five, the age when archbishops usually retire. But the pope wanted Jorge to continue his work in Argentina. So Jorge kept visiting hospitals, prisons, and the Buenos Aires slums. He also preached in favor of things the Church didn't approve of. In his opinion, gay couples should be able to marry— not in a church, but in a government office. He believed this kind of marriage (called a civil union) gave gay people the same rights as other married couples. He also preached that unwed parents should be free to have their children baptized in church. Catholics who wanted the Church to change agreed with Jorge. They saw him as honest, brave, and compassionate. He was a strong leader, and they loved him for it.

Then, on February 11, 2013, surprising news came from Rome: Pope Benedict XVI had decided to resign. It was the first time this had happened since 1294. The announcement came as a shock. But in some ways it made sense. Benedict was eighty-five years old and growing frail. The many scandals surrounding the Church had worried and saddened him. Did they lead to his decision? Nobody knew for sure.

But one thing was certain: The Church needed a new pope. So in March 2013, Cardinal Jorge Bergoglio attended another papal conclave in Rome. As in 2005, there were 114 other cardinals assembling to choose the next pope. As in 2005, huge crowds gathered in St. Peter's Square. Once again everyone waited patiently for the results of the voting that was taking place inside the small chapel. And once again it took a long time.

Finally, on the evening of March 13, a plume of white smoke rose out of the Sistine Chapel chimney. The chapel bells rang out: A new pope had been elected. Hundreds of thousands of people in the rainy square shouted for joy. When they learned who he was, the Argentinians in the crowd waved their country's flag with special pride.

Jorge Mario Bergoglio was the first Jesuit in history to become pope. He was the first pope from Latin America, home to about 40 percent of

the world's 1.2 billion Catholics. And he was the first pope to choose the name Francis, honoring St. Francis of Assisi, who was known for helping the poor.

# Saint Francis of Assisi

Saint Francis was born Francesco di Bernardone in Assisi, Italy, in 1181. He was the son of a wealthy merchant, and not at all saintly in his youth—he dressed well, drank with his friends, and enjoyed himself as much as he could. But after being captured in battle and spending a year in a rat-infested jail, he changed. He stopped drinking and caring about his appearance. He spent every day in an empty church, praying. He dressed in rags and went barefoot. He helped the lepers who lived outside Assisi. (Leprosy is a disease that disfigures skin and bones.) The lepers were shunned and made to live apart, but Francis embraced them. All he wanted was to live in poverty and serve God.

Francis attracted many followers, and together they rebuilt churches, worked for farmers, prayed, and preached. They did not own money or property.

They gave up their families. They were humble and kind to everyone. Francis called all people sisters and brothers. He loved animals, too, and sometimes preached to them. In one well-known story, he persuaded a wolf to stop killing local farm animals, and the wolf held out its paw to Francis in agreement.

By the thirteenth century, thousands of Francis's followers (called Franciscans) were doing the same kind of work in Europe. When he became too weak to work, he named another leader and retreated to the hills near Assisi.

Francis died in 1226 and was made a saint in 1228.

# CHAPTER 7
## A New Day

Pope Francis greeted the world wearing ordinary white robes and a plain cross. "Brothers and sisters, good evening," he said, smiling down at the two hundred thousand rain-soaked, cheering people. After leading them in three prayers— an Our Father, a Hail Mary, and a Glory Be—he said he would go with them on "a journey of brotherhood, of love, and of trust between us."

Normally, the new pope would then bless the crowd. Instead, Pope Francis first asked the crowd to bless him, bowing his head low. His request touched the hearts of countless people—those in the square, and millions more watching on television. The humble, unexpected words hinted that Francis would do things differently from other popes.

And he did, starting immediately.

Instead of taking a limousine, that evening he rode to dinner on a bus with the cardinals who had elected him. (The fact that he did not ride in the Mercedes-Benz "Popemobile" made headlines in newspapers all over the world.)

At dinner, he sat with the cardinals, not above them at a special table.

The next day, after celebrating his first Mass as pope, Pope Francis continued to behave like an ordinary priest. He packed his suitcase and paid his hotel bill. He thanked every person at the hotel who had served him.

He phoned his dentist in Buenos Aires to cancel an appointment. He called his newspaper seller there to stop delivery of the paper. "Seriously, it's

Jorge Bergoglio, I'm calling you from Rome," he told the astonished man.

Later, he was shown the apartments in the Vatican where the pope was supposed to live.

After seeing the huge, formal rooms with their marble floors and heavy furniture, he said, "There's room for three hundred people here. I don't need all this space." With that, he decided to live in a much simpler house that had been used for visiting priests. There were objections— it was a highly unusual choice!—but he insisted.

The pope's bedroom at Casa Santa Marta

That night he phoned his beloved sister, Maria Elena. She was the only member of his family still alive. When she asked him how he felt, he replied, "I'm fine, relax."

Maria Elena

"You looked really good on television—you had a radiant expression," she said. "I wish I could give you a hug."

"We are hugging, we are together," he told her. "I have you very close to my heart."

The down-to-earth way Pope Francis was behaving didn't surprise his sister or his friends in Argentina. They were used to him. But people who didn't know him were amazed. Some were reminded of St. Francis of Assisi, a humble, kind man of the people. Others worried that Francis was not being respectful enough of the papacy. It was, after all, the most important job in the world's oldest and largest church. "We're going to have to get used to a new way of doing things," one Vatican official told journalists.

But most people rejoiced. They felt that by preaching love, mercy, and friendship, Pope

Francis was reminding the world what the Church was really about. With his warm, friendly smile and welcoming manner, he was a breath of fresh air. And though he was seventy-six, he had the energy of a much younger man. This was fortunate, because he had a lot of work to do.

# CHAPTER 8
## A Helping Hand

Pope Francis's first year in office began in March, one of the most important months in the Catholic calendar. In the days leading up to Easter, he led religious ceremonies every day. These included morning Mass at a church near the Vatican, and a parade in the Roman hills on Ash Wednesday. Photographed and televised, these events were seen not only by people in Rome but also by millions around the world.

But one of the most important things the pope did in March 2013 remained a closely guarded secret for more than a year. Soon after he took office, he heard that the United States and Cuba were interested in having a better relationship.

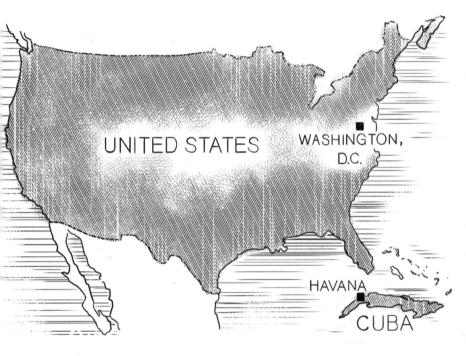

UNITED STATES

WASHINGTON, D.C.

HAVANA

CUBA

The two countries had not been on good terms for more than fifty years. Travel between them was forbidden. So was doing business together.

The pope quickly got in touch with US president Barack Obama and Cuban president Raul Castro, and offered to be their go-between. He would talk first to each of them to see if meetings could take place. Everyone agreed, and a series of secret talks and meetings began. Gradually the meetings grew friendlier. When problems came up, the pope offered solutions.

And within eighteen months, the United States and Cuba were on much better terms. The news became public on December 17, 2014, the pope's seventy-eighth birthday. Both leaders thanked the pope warmly for everything he had done. His quiet, careful work had helped to change history.

Raul Castro

By this time, the world already knew that Pope Francis was an extraordinary man. Beyond his skills as a diplomat, he was a kind, compassionate, outgoing leader. From the first, he had preached that the purpose of the Church was to be merciful. Its mission was to reach out and welcome people, not turn them away. (He once said he would happily baptize a Martian!)

In Rome, as in Buenos Aires, he made a point

of paying special attention to society's outcasts. He gave out phone cards to refugees—people who had fled their own country—so they could call home. He had showers and a shelter built for the homeless. He offered them sleeping bags and made sure they found health care. Time after time, he spoke out on their behalf. "I want a Church that is poor and for the poor," he said.

Pope Francis greeting refugees at the airport.

# CHAPTER 9
## Taking Charge

Pope Francis was also bluntly outspoken about the causes of poverty. He preached against greed in politics and business, and criticized powerful criminals. For those who were used to quieter, more distant pontiffs, Francis came as quite a shock.

However, in his first years of office, he received high praise and dozens of honors. The way he practiced what he preached made Catholics hopeful about the Church's future. They were encouraged by the way he tackled some of its toughest problems.

One of these problems was the Vatican Bank. Located inside the Vatican in a tower that was once a dungeon, it was founded in 1887.

Pope Leo XIII used it like a piggy bank for his treasure, a trunk full of gold coins.

Over the years, the bank became extremely wealthy. There were rumors that it held hundreds of millions of dollars. But only a handful of people knew exactly how much money was in the bank, where it came from, or where exactly it was going. The information was closely guarded.

Pope Francis had long opposed corruption—crooked deals—in business and in government. Faced with corruption inside the Vatican itself, he quickly took action. He set up an investigation that discovered the Vatican Bank had millions in hidden funds.

NEWS    SCANDAL AT VATICAN BANK

The pope then fired most of the bank's officers. He replaced them with people he trusted. Thanks to the pope, the records of the Vatican Bank are now clear and up-to-date. Reform continues, but the bank's worst problems have been solved.

Unfortunately, the task of reforming the Curia—made up of all the people who have Vatican jobs—was much harder. The Curia began in the Middle Ages as a small group of priests who helped the pope. By 2013, it had become a sprawling network of three thousand people. Almost all of them had gotten their jobs through family connections. Curia officials were closely knit and powerful. There were rumors that they were corrupt, too.

The Curia was supposed to run the Vatican and help the pope, but it had often been accused of working against him and helping its members instead. In the past, it kept information from the pope. It kept people from seeing him. And it set up private meetings with him in exchange for favors.

Above all, the Curia guarded its power and

fought change. Pope Benedict had tried to reform it and failed. So had others. "Popes come and go; the Curia is forever" was a well-known saying about it.

Pope Francis made his first attempt at reform quickly. In April 2013, he handpicked a group of nine cardinals from all over the world. Their nickname was C9, and their goal was to simplify the way the Curia worked. This had never been tried before.

The pope also removed some top Curia officials and cut the salaries of others. He announced that high-ranking members had to go with him to a monastery for his yearly retreat. For five days before Easter, he would lead them in a program of prayer.

In case the Curia didn't get the point, Pope Francis lashed out at them in a Christmas 2014 address. They were not doing good work.

They were not good Catholics. And they were much too gloomy. The Curia was shocked and dismayed, especially when the pope's words were reported around the globe.

In other, gentler steps, Pope Francis has limited the Curia's role in his daily life. From the day he took office, he has made many of his own phone calls. When people call him at the Vatican,

he often picks up the phone himself, saying, "Hello, it's Bergoglio." He likes to e-mail people,

and he always chats with them directly, whether
he's in the Vatican cafeteria or St. Peter's Square.
Bypassing the Curia has brought him much closer
to ordinary people, and they are thrilled.

Most people are also very happy about his concern for the environment. In 2015, he devoted a whole encyclical (written statement) to it, which no other pope had ever done. He wrote about climate change, pollution, and recycling. He urged everyone to treat the earth, "our common home," with respect. In the prayers that closed the encyclical, he reminded us that all living creatures need loving care.

ENCYCLICAL LETTER
LAUDATO ST
OF THE HOLY FATHER
FRANCIS
ON CARE FOR OUR COMMON HOME

*All-powerful God,*
*you are present in the whole universe,*
*and in the smallest of your creatures.*
*Pour out upon us the power of your love,*
*that we may protect life and beauty.*
*Fill us with peace, that we may live*
*as brothers and sisters, harming no one.*

# CHAPTER 10
## A Church of the Heart

Pope Francis turned eighty on December 17, 2016. "I have the feeling that my pontificate will be brief," he told one interviewer, "four or five years; I do not know, even two or three . . ."

That was in 2013, and the pope has made many changes to the Church since then. His critics say he hasn't done enough. They say the Curia is still too powerful, that there are still dishonest priests, bishops, and cardinals. And that women are still waiting for a more important role in the Church.

Still, no other pope in memory has done so much in such a short time. He has made the Church friendlier and more open, "a Church of the heart." He has added dozens of cardinals from poorer countries, and countries outside Europe, to the College of Cardinals.

And he has invited all Catholics to voice their opinions on divorce and other issues that are very important to them.

The pope has always been interested in ordinary people of all religions—their daily lives, their feelings, and their human needs. He has said many times that he is just like them, a human being who is far from perfect. Speaking with them in person, and via letters and e-mails, he is down-to-earth, affectionate, and encouraging. "More like a brother than a father," as one friend put it. One journalist wrote that instead of pointing a finger, Pope Francis offers a helping hand.

Millions of people follow the pope every day on Facebook, Twitter, and Instagram. Watching him on their phones and computers, they see what is important to him, because he teaches by example. He doesn't just preach that everyone should care for the poor, he goes out and does it. He lives simply, without pomp or luxury. He washes the feet of drug addicts, embraces the disabled, and kneels to pray with criminals.

He walks around Rome without bodyguards. He is friendly and welcoming, saying, "We are children of the same God, who want to live in peace." Like St. Francis of Assisi, Pope Francis is showing what true faith means. He is inspiring people to become better.

And they will cherish him for it, no matter what else he accomplishes.

# Pope Francis Firsts

- Pope Francis is the first Jesuit pope and the first pope from South America.

- He is the first pope to take the name Francis.

- He is the first pope with 11 million Twitter followers, a Facebook page, and an Instagram account.

- He is the first pope to wash the feet of a woman.

- He is the first pope to excommunicate the Mafia—that means these crime figures can no longer be part of the Catholic Church.

- He is the first pope to take selfies.

- He is the first pope to build a shelter for the homeless in Rome, and the first to spend his birthday with them.

- He is the first pope to say that he does not judge gay people.

- He is the first pope to write an encyclical—a letter to all the Church bishops—about the dangers of climate change.

# Timeline of Pope Francis's Life

| | |
|---|---|
| 1936 | Born on December 17 in Buenos Aires, Argentina |
| 1955 | Begins studies at a Jesuit seminary |
| 1957 | Undergoes lung surgery after a severe illness |
| 1958 | Begins Jesuit novitiate |
| 1969 | Ordained as a Jesuit priest |
| 1973 | Appointed Jesuit provincial superior for Argentina and Uruguay |
| 1980–1986 | Rector of Colegio Maximo during the last years of the "Dirty War" |
| 1992 | Appointed auxiliary bishop of Buenos Aires |
| 1998 | Becomes archbishop of Buenos Aires |
| 2001 | Made a cardinal by Pope John Paul II |
| | Begins weekly visits to hospital patients with HIV in Buenos Aires |
| 2002–2003 | Leads talks between citizens' groups and politicians during Argentina's financial crisis |
| 2005 | Takes part in the election of Pope Benedict XVI |
| 2013 | Elected pope on March 23 |
| | Takes the name Francis |
| 2014 | Authorizes investigation of the Vatican Bank |
| 2015 | Visits Africa for five days |
| | Says Mass for six million in the Philippines |
| | Invites homeless into the Vatican for his birthday |
| 2016 | Declares Mother Teresa a saint |

# Timeline of the World

| | |
|---|---|
| **1935** | Regina Jonas, first woman rabbi, ordained in Germany |
| **1939** | Italy becomes Nazi Germany's ally in World War II |
| **1943** | Benito Mussolini dies |
| | Italy allies itself with the United States, England, and France to fight Germany |
| **1961** | John F. Kennedy becomes the first Catholic president of US |
| **1962** | Vatican II begins in Rome |
| **1963** | John F. Kennedy is assassinated |
| **1965** | Vatican II ends |
| | Nuns may choose to wear habits or street clothes |
| | Jorge Luis Borges gets his sixth nomination for the Nobel Prize in Literature |
| **1968** | Robert F. Kennedy is assassinated |
| | Jesuit priest Daniel Berrigan leads Catholic clergy in protesting the Vietnam War |
| **1973** | Juan Perón is elected president of Argentina |
| **1978** | Karol Wojtyla becomes Pope John Paul II |
| **1979– 1983** | Argentina's "Dirty War" |
| **2005** | Benedict XVI becomes pope |
| **2007** | Cristina Fernandez de Kirchner is the first woman to be elected president of Argentina |
| **2012** | The Curia's corruption is revealed |
| **2013** | Pope Benedict XVI resigns |

# Bibliography

**\* Books for young readers**

Acocella, Joan. "Rich Man, Poor Man: The Radical Visions of St. Francis,"
*New Yorker*, January 14, 2013.

Allen, John L., Jr. *The Catholic Church: What Everyone Needs to Know*.
New York: Oxford University Press, 2014.

Carroll, James. "Who Am I to Judge?: A Radical Pope's First Year,"
*New Yorker*, December 23 and 30, 2013.

Collins, Father Michael. *Pope Francis: A Photographic Portrait of the
People's Pope*. New York: DK Publishing, 2015.

Duffy, Eamon. "Who Is the Pope?" *New York Review of Books*,
February 19, 2015.

Ivereigh, Austen. *The Great Reformer: Francis and the Making of a
Radical Pope*. New York: Henry Holt, 2014.

Klein, Christopher. "Ten Things You May Not Know About the Vatican,"
History.com, March 12, 2013, http://www.history.com/news/10-things-
you-may-not-know-about-the-vatican.

\* Kramer, Barbara. *Pope Francis*. Washington, DC: National Geographic
Kids Readers, 2015.

* Machajewski, Sarah. ***Pope Francis: The People's Pontiff***. New York: Britannica Educational Publishing, 2015.

Trigilio, Rev. John, Jr., and Rev. Kenneth Brighenti. ***Catholicism for Dummies***. Hoboken, NJ: John Wiley & Sons, 2012.

Vallely, Paul. ***Pope Francis: Untying the Knots***. London: Bloomsbury Publishing, 2013.

* Watson, Stephanie. ***Pope Francis: First Pope from the Americas***. Minneapolis, MN: Lerner Publications, 2014.

## Websites

w2.Vatican.va

www.catholic.com

www.catholicherald.co.uk

www.jesuits.org

www.religionnews.com